Gathering
At
Golgotha

Readers' Theater
For Good Friday

Katherine Bailey Babb

CSS Publishing Company, Inc., Lima, Ohio

Copyright © 2001 by
CSS Publishing Company, Inc.
Lima, Ohio

For more information about CSS Publishing Company resources, visit our website at www.csspub.com.

ISBN 0-7880-1791-8   PRINTED IN U.S.A.

For my husband Jeff,
my partner and
"balancer."

Notes

Readers:
Narrator 1
Narrator 2
Narrator 3 (also voice of Jesus)
Mary, the mother of Jesus
Mary Magdalene
Peter
John, the beloved disciple

Costumes:
None

Setting:
The three narrators should be on one side of the stage at a podium, and the four characters should be on the other side. If they are also the singers, they should all group at one side or the other (probably next to the piano or organ) when they sing. If a separate choir is to sing, they should stand in the middle.

Songs:
"The Old Rugged Cross" (Congregation)
"He Never Said A Mumbalin' Word"
"Were You There?"
"Go To Dark Gethsemane"
"Please Don't Leave Us"
"O Sacred Head Now Wounded"
(Note: all songs except "Please Don't Leave Us" are found in most hymnals. See pages 20-26 of this book for words and music for "Please Don't Leave Us")

Props:
Two large candelabra, one on each side of the stage. Readers need personal flashlights or small lights at the podium. (Same for the organist/pianist and choir if separate from the readers.)

Sound Effects:
Thunder
Earthquake
Screams (if desired)
Huge ripping sound

Gathering At Golgotha

(Stage lights are on, but low. All the candles should be lighted by the speakers as they come on stage. Narrators 1, 2, and 3 are on one side of the stage and share a microphone; Mary, Mary Magdalene, John, and Peter are on the other side. Overhead spotlight on Narrators.)

Narrator 1: We welcome those of you who have come tonight to share the remembrance of the death of our Lord. As Christians, we have the knowledge of Jesus' resurrection from the dead, and in our hearts we have hope. But tonight let us share the story from the perspective of those who were part of this drama, and hear the words they might have said as the person who was nearest and dearest to their hearts was ripped away from them and nailed to a cross.

Narrator 2: Let us pray. Heavenly Father, thank you for this time to gather here to remember the events surrounding the death of Jesus. We thank you for the gift of his resurrection, and the love and grace that is available to us because of his death and resurrection.

Narrator 3: Please stand and turn to page ___, and sing with us "The Old Rugged Cross," verses 1 and 4.

(Congregation sings.)

Narrator 1: Now when morning had come, all the chief priests and the elders of the people took counsel against Jesus to put him to death; and they bound him, and led him away, and delivered him up to Pilate the governor. The governor questioned him saying,

Narrator 2: "Are you the King of the Jews? Are you the Messiah?"

Narrator 3: And Jesus answered, "You have said so."

Narrator 2: Then the chief priests and the other Jewish leaders made their accusations against him, and

Narrator 3: Jesus said nothing.

Narrator 1: Then Pilate asked, "Don't you hear the terrible things the leaders of the Jews have said against you? They think you are a blasphemer — one who says he is equal to God! Don't you have anything to say for yourself?"

Narrator 2: Jesus did not answer him about any of the charges, and Pilate was amazed.

Song: "He Never Said A Mumbalin' Word" (verse 1)

Narrator 3: Now the governor's custom was to release one Jewish prisoner each year during the Passover celebration — any one they wanted. This year there was a particularly notorious criminal in jail named Barabbas. And as the crowds gathered that morning, Pilate asked them, "Which shall I release to you, Barabbas or Jesus who is called Christ?" Pilate knew that it was because of envy of Jesus' popularity with the people that the Jews had handed Jesus over to him.

Narrator 1: But the chief priests and the elders had persuaded the people to ask for the release of Barabbas, and the death of Jesus. The crowds roared:

All Readers: "Give us Barabbas! Give us Barabbas!"

Narrator 2: Pilate answered, "What shall I do with this man, Jesus, your Messiah?" And the crowd, in a riot frenzy, cried,

All Readers: "Crucify him! Crucify him! We have no King but Caesar!"

Narrator 3: And Pilate, seeing that a riot was beginning and that he wasn't getting anywhere, sent for a bowl of water and washed his hands in front of the whole mob, saying, "I am innocent of the blood of this good man. The responsibility is yours!"

Narrator 1: And the crowd answered,

All Readers: "His blood be on us and on our children!"

Narrator 2: Then Pilate released Barabbas to them. And after he had scourged Jesus, he gave Jesus to his Roman soldiers to be crucified.

Narrator 3: Then the governor's soldiers took Jesus into the praetorium, their armory, and called out the whole contingent of soldiers.

Narrator 1: They stripped him and put a scarlet robe on him. They made a crown from long thorns and put it on his head, and placed a stick in his right hand as a scepter and knelt before him in mockery. They yelled at him, saying,

All Readers: "Good health to you! Long life to you, King of the Jews!"

Narrator 2: And they spat on him, and grabbed the stick and beat him on the head with it. And after they had mocked him, they stripped him of the robe, covered with his blood from the scourging, and put his own clothes back on him and led him away to crucify him.

Narrator 3: Then they went out to an area known as Golgotha, Calvary in Latin, which means "the place of a skull."

Narrator 1: And two others also, who were criminals, were being led away to be put to death with him. And when they came to the place called Golgotha, there they crucified him and the criminals, one on the right and the other on the left. But Jesus said,

Narrator 3 (Jesus): "Father, forgive them, for they know not what they do."

(*Lights on Singers*)

Song: "Were You There?" (verses 1, 2, 3)

(*Lights on Narrators*)

Narrator 2: At a distance, watching all this, were Jesus' mother, Mary; Mary Magdalene; Peter and the young disciple, John; and others who had been friends, acquaintances, disciples, and supporters of Jesus during the three years of his ministry. Let's listen to what may have been their conversation.

(*Lights on Characters*)

Mary Magdalene: I can't believe that we are standing here today, actually watching him die! What happened to us? For so long, we were all together, traveling with Jesus, watching and listening, learning to live as God's own children, and now ... *this!*

Mary: Yes, Mary Magdalene, I know. You were one of many of those blessed to have been given a new life. There is no resemblance now to the haunted, pain-ridden woman you were before my Son touched you and set you free.

Peter: He touched us all in so many ways. I can still remember the day I met him. He came to my house, healed my wife's mother, and sat down to supper with us. He was comfortable wherever he was. Not that I was always too comfortable with him. I was too astonished even to stand up that day when he caused so many fish to swim into my nets. Just the first of many times when I didn't know what to say, or said the wrong thing.

John: Peter, don't be too hard on yourself. At least you always tried to do and say what you thought he wanted. Remember the time you tried to walk on the water, just like Jesus?

Peter: I almost did it. *Almost* ... that seems to be my byword ... My friends, I need to tell you about last night.

Mary: Yes, exactly what *did* happen last night? You men all left and went to the garden. Then we found out he had been arrested, and followed the mobs.

Mary Magdalene: It was Judas, wasn't it? I could feel that something was wrong with him, somehow. He was so unhappy lately.

John: Yes, he was the one who betrayed Jesus, by *kissing* him! How could he? All I know is that we were with Jesus, in the garden. He went away from us to pray, and asked us to pray, too. But I guess I fell asleep. I don't know how I could sleep; we all knew the religious leaders were furious with Jesus about cleansing the temple and calling it a den of robbers. It was too dangerous, really, to sleep. But I did.

Peter: We all fell asleep, John. I woke up for a little while and I could see him, all alone, praying and weeping as if his heart were breaking. He seemed to be asking God to "take a cup from him." He was sweating so hard it seemed like drops of blood were coming down his face. He was in so much distress. He was always praying. The day we were on the mountain and we saw him in shining robes with Moses and Elijah, he was praying. He got up early every morning to pray. But this was different. He was in pure agony.

Song: "Go To Dark Gethsemane" (verse 1)

Mary: Don't you understand? He knew what would happen last night and this morning. He must have prayed to be spared all this pain.

Mary Magdalene: Can you blame him? It is tearing me apart to watch him like this. Mary, I wish you would leave this place. You should never have come. The crowd has been so bloodthirsty. This all feels so awful. The Roman soldiers are scary, but not as scary as the crowd. It seems they *enjoy* seeing people die like this.

Mary: Magdalene, where else could I be? But you're right, this does all seem like a nightmare. Seeing nails piercing the hands of my Son, seeing him bleed like this ... this holy and beautiful man, whose life and words and love touched us all, from the oldest to the youngest, even the children who piled on his lap in noisy, giggling heaps ... to watch his agony. You're right, Mary, I wish I did not have to be here. (*Pauses*) But even when I was the happiest, and my Son was a tiny baby, a part of me knew that something like this would happen.

Mary Magdalene: Really, Mary? What do you mean?

Mary: When Joseph and I took Jesus to the temple as a baby, to carry out the customs of the law, a holy man named Simeon took my tiny Son into his arms and said words to me that I have never been able to forget.

(*Lights off Characters and over to Narrators*)

Narrator 3: Behold, this Child is appointed for the fall and rise of many in Israel, and for a sign to be opposed, and a sword will pierce even your own soul — to the end that thoughts from many hearts will be revealed.

(*Lights back to Characters*)

Mary Magdalene: (*Bitterly*) "Hearts to be revealed" — ha! Just listen to the people around you; their hearts are full of murder and cursing. The soldiers are casting lots for his robe — the special one you made him, Mary, without seams. But the mob really is worse. Listen to them. How can they say such things?

(*Lights to Narrators*)

Narrator 1: (*Very sarcastically*) Look at him! He saved others; let him save himself if this is the Christ of God, the chosen one!

Narrator 2: (*Sarcastically*) See, Jesus! Your sign says, "This is the King of the Jews!" If you really are the King of the Jews, save yourself!

Narrators 1 and 2: Save yourself!

(*Lights to Characters*)

John: He could, you know. He could save himself, even now.

Mary Magdalene: Save himself? From *this*? Why would you say that?

John: Mary Magdalene, weren't you listening to him? He knew that this was coming; he kept trying to warn us, but we couldn't hear what he was saying. He kept trying to tell us that he was going away. He even talked once about being crucified, just before we all came in to Jerusalem last week.

Peter: He always talked about his kingdom. His *kingdom*! And some of us were conceited and crazy enough to ask him if we could sit at his right and left hand in his kingdom. Look at who is at his right and left hands now — common criminals. Can you hear what they are saying?

(*Lights on Narrators*)

Narrator 1: You fool, Jesus! You thought you were somebody, didn't you? And now, look at you. Hanging here on a cross just like me, and this other piece of human trash. If you really were someone, you would get yourself off this cross, and save us, too!

Narrator 2: Hush, you! Don't you even fear God when you are hanging here dying? At least you and I deserve to die for the things

13

we have done, but this man has done nothing to deserve what is happening to him. Jesus — Jesus, please remember me when you come in your kingdom.

Narrator 3 (Jesus): Truly, I say to you, today you shall be with me in paradise.

(*Lights on Characters*)

John: Did you hear that? He said that criminal would be with him — today — in paradise.

Mary: Yes, I heard. He came from the Father and is returning to the Father.

Mary Magdalene: I'm sorry. I just can't bear it. He *can't* leave us! I was nothing before I knew him. The first time I laid eyes on him, there in the pharisee's house, all I could do was weep. I wept all over his feet, and had nothing to wipe his feet with but my hair. He changed my life — he made me a whole person again! What will I — what will we all — do without him?

Peter: Mary Magdalene, you're feeling what we all feel. When we walked with him, and listened to him — well, when he said that the Father knew each sparrow that fell, I believed it. The man could touch a leper and heal him, make blind men see and lame men walk.

John: Yes, Peter. You could feel his power before he came into a room. But he kept his reasons to himself. Even when he raised Lazarus from the dead, I could never understand why he hadn't come earlier and made him well. Then maybe the leaders would not have felt that they had to kill him.

Mary: John, I feel at this moment more anguish than I can say. But we can't know Jesus' mind, or the mind of the Father. All we can do is hope and trust.

Peter: I still haven't told you about the rest of the night. At dinner, Jesus had told me that he was praying for me, for my strength not to fail.

John: Yes, I heard him say that.

Peter: Did you hear the rest? He added that before the cock crowed this morning I would deny him three times. I said I would *never* deny him. But I did.

John: It was so awful when the crowd came to get him though, Peter. We were all terrified. Here we had been in the temple day after day, and then they came to arrest him in the night like some dangerous criminal. But I saw you follow him to the house of Caiaphas, and stand outside the door.

Peter: Yes, I followed. But I acted like a fool and a coward. There he was, my leader, my Lord, my ... friend, sitting there being questioned and beaten like some evil man. I had tried to fight against them, there in the garden, with my sword, but that hadn't worked. I felt so helpless, so desperate. Half of me was screaming with rage and the other half was shaking with fear. When they asked me who I was ... I ... it was just that I was so scared. I denied I ever knew him! Not once, but three times!

Mary: (*Sympathetically*) Oh, Peter ...

Peter: But the worst was when he looked at me. He heard me say that I didn't know him, and then he looked at me. Then I heard a rooster, and remembered what he said — he knew what I would do! Can I ever raise my head again? And now I'll never get to tell him how sorry I am.

John: Peter, I don't know how, but I know that this can't be the end. He always tried to warn us this would happen. And he did raise Lazarus and others from the dead. Maybe, if we just trust ...

Mary Magdalene: I'm not sure I *can* trust. All I want is for everything to be like it was: miracles on the hillside, sermons by the lake, conversations around the fireside as we traveled around. I want to hear him laughing again. And telling us stories that we don't quite understand. I want to see people's faces as they hear him speaking their names.

Mary: Magdalene, no one wants him to die. What will we do without him?

(*Lights to Singers*)

Song: "Please Don't Leave Us" (or "Go To Dark Gethsemane")

(*Sound effects: thunder, lights go on and off and on again. Narrators extinguish candles*)

John: Mary, Peter, what is happening? What's going on?

(*Lights go out; Readers et al use flashlights*)

Narrator 1: Now from the sixth hour there was darkness over all the land until the ninth hour. And about the ninth hour Jesus cried with a loud voice.

Narrator 3 (Jesus): "My God, my God, why have you forsaken me?"

Narrator 2: Some of the bystanders said, "He's calling Elijah," and one of them tried to give him vinegar to drink. But the others said, "Wait, let's see whether Elijah will come to save him."

Narrator 1: And Jesus cried again with a loud voice and gave up his spirit.

Narrator 3 (Jesus): "Father, into thy hands I commit my spirit. It is finished."

(*Sound effects: thunder or earthquake; a huge ripping sound; women screaming*)

Narrator 2: (*Concurrently over the sound effects*) And behold, the curtain of the Temple protecting the Holy of Holies was ripped in two, from top to bottom. And the earth shook, and the rocks were split. The tombs were also opened, and many bodies of the saints who had fallen asleep were raised, coming out of their tombs.

(*Cease sound effects*)

Narrator 1: When the centurion and those who were with him, keeping watch over Jesus, saw the earthquake and everything that was happening, they were filled with awe, and exclaimed:

All Readers: "Surely this was the Son of God!"

Mary Magdalene: Mary, hold my hand! This blackness is terrifying. There are so many strange sounds. He — he's really dead, isn't he?

John: He's really dead. He was right to fear this, to sweat drops of blood. The light has gone out of the world with his death.

Mary Magdalene: What do we do now?

Mary: This man was my Son. When Jesus was alive he touched our hearts, healed our pain, and held our hands. He comforted our tears, and made us know that we were completely loved and understood. And even in this darkness, the light may yet return.

Peter: Please, God, Abba, Father, please ... don't let this be the end!

(*Lights partially up — on the sides only, not front*)

Song: "O Sacred Head Now Wounded"

Narrator 1: Heavenly Father, we thank you that you loved the world so much that you allowed your Son to die a horrible and painful death on the cross. At times, when we are alone or sick or grieving or in pain, we feel that we cannot see or touch the light of Jesus in our lives. Please remind us at those times that Jesus became a man — a human being, like us — and that he knows every emotion that we can experience.

Narrator 2: Thank you for the love that transcends death and pain. Help us to hope for the light, to pray for its return, and to be part of that light as we go out to serve your people. In the name of Jesus, Amen.

Narrator 3: Please feel free to stay and pray if you wish. Then leave this place silently, and reflect on the life and death of our Lord. Prepare your hearts on this day to be open to the resurrection of Jesus, to new life and new hope that is a free gift of God. This Good Friday service is ended. Go in peace.

Please Don't Leave Us
Words and Music by Katherine V. Babb (©1994)

CHORUS
Please don't leave us, please don't leave us.
We have walked by your side, shared your fire at night,
And now, Lord, if you die, there will be no more light
And no place we can hide. Please don't go!

Verse 1
You have called us from jobs and from fam'lies.
We were so glad to follow your lead.
But today when we see you there nailed to that tree —
Can't you do something? Please, Lord, don't die!   CHORUS

Verse 2
When the storm rocked our boat, you said, "Quiet,"
And the winds and the waves did your will.
Now there's screaming and horror and riots —
Stop them killing you here on this hill!   CHORUS

Verse 3
When we walked thru' the country together,
You made each act of life show God's grace.
Now you're bound up with nails and with leather;
We can't bear all this pain on your face.

CHORUS
Please don't leave us, please don't leave us.
We have walked by your side, shared your fire at night,
And now, Lord, if you die, there will be no more light
And no place we can hide. Please don't go!
Please don't go!

Please Don't Leave Us

Words and Music by Katherine V. Babb

Slowly

CHORUS: Please don't leave us, please don't leave us. We have walked by your side, shared your fi- re at night, and now, Lord, if you die, there will be no more light, and no place we can hide;

11
Verse 1
Bb C
Please don't go! You have
13 F C Bb
called us from jobs and from fam'- lies. We were
15 F C
so glad to fol- low your lead. But to-
17 Dm A
day when we see you there nailed to that tree-- Can't you
19 Dm Gm A Dm
do some- thing? Please, Lord, don't die! CHORUS Please don't

© Katherine V. Babb 1994

Please Don't Leave Us

leave us! Please don't leave us! We have

walked by your side, shared your fi- re at night, and now

Lord, if you die, there will be no more light, and no

place we can hide; Please don't go! *Verse 2:*

When the storm rocked our boat, you said,

© *Katherine V. Babb 1994*

Please Don't Leave Us

31 Bb ... F

"Qui- et," and the winds and the waves did your

33 C ... Dm

will. Now there's scream-ing and hor- ror and

35 A ... Dm ... Gm

ri- ots--- Stop them kill- ing you here on this

37 A ... Dm ... Gm

hill! CHORUS Please don't leave us! Please don't

39 Dm

leave us. We have walked by your side, shared your

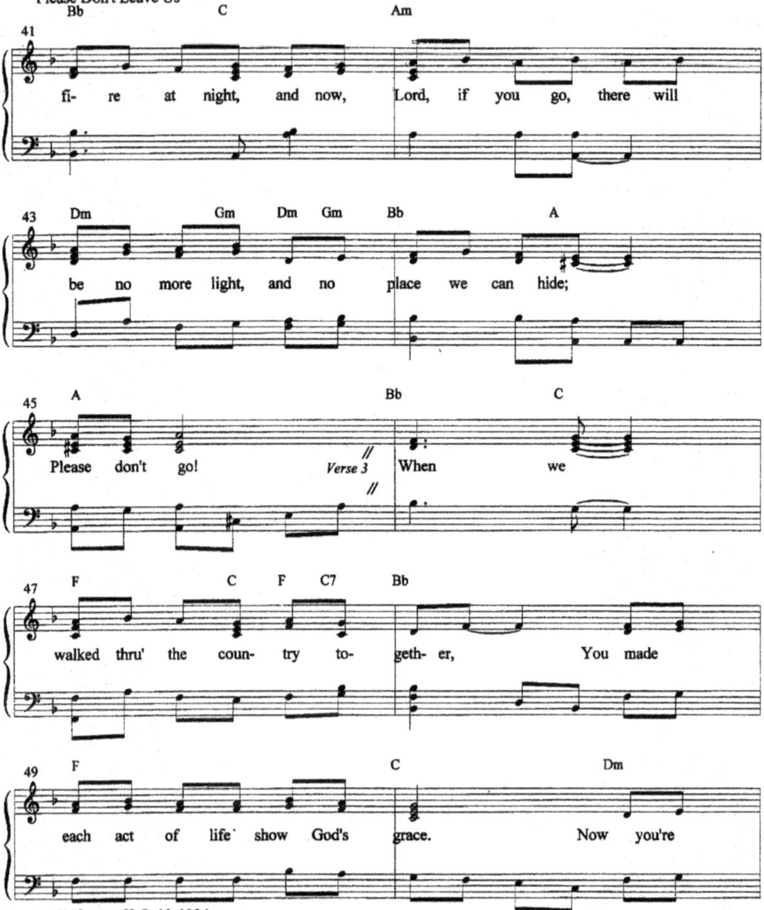

Katherine V. Babb 1994

bound up with nails and with leath-er; We can't

bear all this pain on your face. Please don't

leave us, please don't leave us. We have

walked by your side, shared your fi- re at night, and now

Lord, if you die, there will be no more light, and no

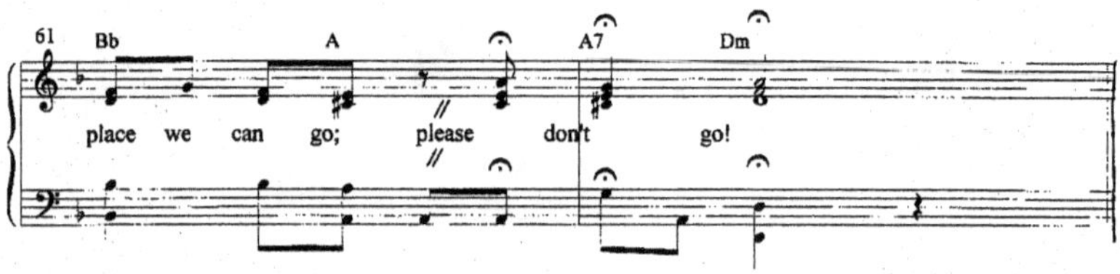
61
Bb
A
A7
Dm
place we can go; please don't go!

www.ingramcontent.com/pod-product-compliance
Lightning Source LLC
Chambersburg PA
CBHW071808020426
42331CB00008B/2447